AYURVEDA DEMYSTIFIED

FOR OPTIMUM WESTERN LIVING

3rd Edition

GAYLE REDFERN

1603 Capitol Ave, Suite 310 A275 Cheyenne, Wyoming 82001
Office: (307) 459-1803 | Fax: (307) 224-8450
Website: www.authoraide.com

CONTENTS

PREFACE

During my prior career as a Health Practitioner and Counselor, I used various techniques with clients to correct or explain health and emotional issues. However, these became inadequate. There were some people experiencing mysterious difficulties. Others might experience a symptom one day and be fine the next day without explanation. Consequently, I searched for answers.

My interest in Eastern cultures led me to explore their medical systems. What I discovered were systems that had the potential of healing without drugs or surgical treatments. They acknowledged imbalances and offered solutions that were drug free.

As I learned more about Ayurveda, I discovered it not only counteracts imbalances but encourages the individual to take more responsibility for their health. In addition it outlines a daily regime for each person.

Ayurveda is a very complex science of life when it is studied in detail and followed in its entirety. However, a person can study segments and achieve success with that particular piece. For myself, I discovered that by slightly adjusting my diet, I was able to eliminate aches and pains from my own body.

With the new knowledge, my next steps were to use it in my practice, teach workshops, write a booklet to accompany the classes and finally write this small book.

This book is possibly the first step for many individuals into the world of Ayurveda. It introduces the concepts in English terms. I hope that once the reader has become comfortable with this information, they move on and learn much more. I believe it truly is a gateway to healthy living.

I. INTRODUCTION

Ayurveda (Sanskrit for "science of life") is possibly the oldest health science, approximately 5,000 years old, predating and influencing most medical systems. It is a comprehensive system combining natural therapies with a personalized approach to treatments. Historically, it was the only system practiced in India.

Unfortunately, when British rulers suppressed Indian practices, it was relegated to Grandma's kitchen and rural communities. Gradually however, leaders in India, recognizing the strengths of both Western medicine and Ayurveda, amalgamated the knowledge, thus producing a complex and powerful system of healthy living.

For someone raised in a Western culture, Ayurveda can be best defined as a preventative science while Western medicine is corrective. The modern Ayurvedic doctor believes there are five ways to health:

Meditation:	Let the body heal itself
Diet:	Take in what the body will use best
Herbs:	Let nature provide what is needed
Chemical Drugs:	Use what Western science has given us
Surgery:	Remove what is non-functional

Meditation, diet and herbs are mainly preventive procedures while the use of herbs, drugs and surgery are corrective. While numerous systems follow this preventive and corrective classification, Ayurveda differs by combining five abroad principles. One, it places equal emphasis on our body, mind and spirit, restoring the inherent harmony of the individual. Two, it incorporates the elements earth, air, water, fire and ether. Three, it follows a circadian system. Four, it understands the three life-force energies existing within all life forms. Finally, it recognizes the **balance** that must be part of our internal and external lives. Balance allows us to integrate the hemispheres of our brain, reduce stress, maintain health, and enjoy life around us wherever we live.

After visiting India, Carl Jung commented that, "Life in India had not yet withdrawn into the capsule of the head. It is still the whole body that lives." This is the concept that we must incorporate into our lives, in the commercial word of today. We are not individual pieces of machinery; every part affects other parts and the whole. We live and work in a left-brain society. Spending too much time in the left-brain leaves other parts idle and stagnant. Ayurveda looks at the WHOLE UNIQUE PERSON, emphasizing the interaction of mind, body and spirit. Proponents of Ayurveda believe that illness and disease come from a loss of connection between our body mechanisms, our biological memory and our ability to heal ourselves. They also come from not maintaining the balance according to the three life-force energies operating within us.

These energy forces control everything in nature, ebbing and flowing with the moon cycles, times of day and the seasons. The system is complex and often difficult to follow in our busy lives. To follow the routine of Ayurveda, we would have get up early, meditate at a set time, and eat specific foods at regular times. We would have to be very aware of all fluctuations of the energy flows throughout nature. Much as we would all like to follow this rigorous health regime, it is difficult in our busy commercial world.

I am sure that many are wondering why they should bother to read any further. For the scholar, this book will be incomplete; other books tell the entire story.

What this book does is guide you through the discovery of yourself without spending seven years studying a health system from another country. As I said before, everyone already has three invisible life energies managing our internal operation; it is just the blend that differs. Through knowing your body's composition, you will recognize when you have tilted off balance. This book shows you how to identify the energy forces, plus gives simple techniques to return to a balance.

Another benefit is being able to recognize the dominant energy forces of others as a way to improve your communication and negotiating skills. For example, you may be a person who moves rapidly, is very decisive and yet forgets information as quickly as it is learned. Your partner on the other hand is slower, analyzes all options and remembers details for a long time. These two images are at opposite ends of a spectrum – frustrating for each one and yet, together, they form a powerful team.

A few years ago, I discovered that some of the students in my workshops were overwhelmed learning all those "strange, foreign words." These words became barriers and, even though they liked the philosophy, it stopped them from moving forward. Consequently, I simplified the information, and replaced the Sanskrit terms with English words and phrases.

Initially, I will explain the principles by matching the traditional names with their new counterpart. This is for the benefit of those who want to continue their study. Thereafter, I will use Western terms. While some detail is lost, these adjustments still give the reader more than enough information to understand who they are, how they feel when they are in balance and, more importantly, how they feel when they are off balance. Diet and simple lifestyle adjustments are usually all that is needed to correct the situation.

II. PHILOSOPHY

According to Ayurveda, there are three invisible humours or energy forces flowing throughout all life. Each energy force has one responsibility and protects one general area of the body. These regions are the first area where an imbalance or illness is likely to occur.

The first energy, MOVEMENT force, is responsible for all movement within the entity. It protects the lower part of the torso, pelvic area, large intestine, bones and thighs. The second energy, PROCESSING force, looks after digestion and the fire in the body. It protects the middle part of the torso, small intestine, stomach, sweat glands and blood. Lastly, the STORAGE force, decides what is needed and what needs to be stored for the future. This can be an idea or a vitamin. Its home is the upper part of the torso, heart, lungs, chest, ear, sinuses, nose and mouth. These areas of control are where you first see illness. Nevertheless, imbalances will appear anywhere in the body whenever a particular force is involved.

For example, the STORAGE energy force resides in the chest, where a particular ailment might be a congestive cough. However, even though joints are generally the responsibility of the MOVEMENT energy force, inflammation in a knee is recognized as an excess of the STORAGE energy force.

One of the simplest ways to think of these forces is to imagine three invisible, distinct and clear fluids vibrating and flowing through the entire body. These *doshas,* or humours, are VATA – to us known as the MOVEMENT energy, PITTA - known as the PROCESSING energy, and KAPHA - known as the STORAGE energy. When an imbalance occurs, the fluid of a specific energy force might become muddy, excessive or diminished. This is what we want to correct. Regardless of the dominance of any energy force, the characteristics are consistent. A balanced MOVEMENT force is slow, thin and irregular. Out of balance, it speeds up, becoming more erratic. We can compare it to a serpent or snake slithering away. When the imbalance is large, the *snake* moves faster. A balanced PROCESSING force is strong and lively. Out of balance, it seems like a jumping frog; is the *frog* jumping casually or frenetically? The STORAGE force should feel strong and wide, giving a sense of "floating along" like a swan. Again, when this is out of balance, it is still strong but now flows lethargically, almost as if blocked. Many writers use these animals as analogies. I like them because they display the circular dependency we have. No one animal or force is better or more important than another is. All are necessary and supportive of the others. It is this analogy that I chose for the cover of the book.

For those who are familiar with Native American animal characteristics, you will appreciate the interplay of these three animals with the cardinal in the centre of the circle.

The **cardinal** is known for its beautiful red feathers. He demonstrates renewed vitality and the importance of recognizing your own achievements. Vitality comes from the ever-present energy of all the other three in balance.

The **snake** demonstrates rebirth, initiation and wisdom. He reminds us that the MOVEMENT energy force continually renews itself, initiates new ideas and shows the wisdom of the past. Without movement, we would die.

The **frog** is transformation. We must transform, or PROCESS, before something becomes useful. It links the two extreme energies within us. The frog also reminds us to put out the fire of the PROCESSING by drinking plenty of water. Another way of looking at it is through language. A single word means little until you combine several words into a sentence - until they are processed.

The last animal is the **swan**. The swan, in its slow, graceful beauty, reminds us to awaken the true splendor and power of ourselves. He reminds us to acknowledge everything we have within us, regardless of the image. This magnificent bird completes the circle of energies that flow internally.

As you can see, a body cannot function without vitality (cardinal), continual renewal and wisdom (snake), evolution through life (frog) and the reminder of who we are as an individual (swan). We need the balance of all.

It is important to remember that every activity or function throughout nature and within each life form has all three forces. There may be one force displayed more prominently than another but all three are still present. What makes us different and unique is the combination. One person may have a percentage ratio of 45 - 35 - 20. Another person may have 10 - 25 - 65. We are truly distinctive individuals.

Western science places the emphasis on the ailment, assuming that cold, as an example, affects everyone the same. Therefore, the remedy is the same for all. Because Eastern science looks at the amount of the energy forces present and acknowledges the differences between humans, they notice how the cold affects each differently and respond accordingly. Continuing our example, if a body is predominantly a dry energy type, there wouldn't be as much mucus with the cold. On the other hand, if a body is already carrying moist energy, the cold would increase the moisture content even higher in the form of mucus. This example shows one of the essential details that mark the difference between Western and Eastern science.

To benefit from Ayurveda, it may not be necessary to remember exactly where the forces dominate. It is however, necessary to understand who you are and how everything may affect you. Then, you can take steps to adjust your lifestyle to remain healthy.

Just when you think you are beginning to understand the concepts, you discover there is more. In addition to internal forces, all life follows a cycle as these energies ebb and flow. It is the balance of the three forces and working with the cycles that produce a healthy body.

Seasons

First of all, the seasons of the year are easy to connect with the energy forces because of similar descriptions. When a season displays certain characteristics, we know that a particular energy force is the prevailing force.

The **MOVEMENT** force is light, cool and dry; a cool wind blowing in the fall months. It is also in the fall months when we *move* things into storage for the winter.

The **PROCESSING** force is hot, light and dry. This reminds us of summer, the season when the growth *process* occurs.

The **STORAGE** force is cold, heavy and damp. This reminds us of the winter months. This is the season when we depend upon *stored* goods.

Age

The next cycle of the energy force flows through the ages of individuals.

A baby or young child is soft, plump - *storing* information and nutrients for future needs. The illnesses of childhood are usually congestive - colds, mucus, and flu. Consequently, the STORAGE energy is abundant in the years of youth.

During the teens and adulthood, everything is busy being *processed* by the individual. This is a time for ulcers and skin disorders such as acne. Any ailment that can be associated with fire is likely to occur during these ages, caused by PROCESSING abundance.

These last stage is the abundance of the MOVEMENT force. Since this force is light, fast and airy, it begins to slow down at this time. I call it "the tired phase." Most ailments involve nervous disorders or blockages. The memory information isn't *moving*. The Joints have excess air, causing arthritis. The skin is dry, hence more wrinkles than laugh - lines.

Time of Day

It can be very difficult to incorporate the daily cycles into our daily routine. However, understanding the logic encourages you to plan your day around peaks and valleys of the cycle. For example, doesn't it make sense to follow fitness regime at a time when you have more energy? Wouldn't it be easier to study or solve a mental problem when your mental processing energy is at its peak? The energy forces shift on a four - hour cycle, repeating once during 24 hours. The following is an ideal schedule:

6am to 10am

Rising at a time when the body is relaxed and calm and STORAGE energy is high.

10am to 2pm

Exerting physical stamina, digesting the largest meal when PROCESSING energy is high.

2pm to 6pm

Nervous energy is highest, and MOVEMENT energy is high.

6pm to 10pm

Enjoying a relaxed, slow, evening when the STORAGE energy is high.

10pm to 2am

Warmth of high PROCESSING energy takes you into night.

2am to 6am

Time for dream action - REM dreams, MOVEMENT energy high.

In the following layout, you can see the merging of cycles, seasons, day and age. I have abbreviated the three energy forces as follows

M = MOVEMENT
P = PROCESSING
S = STORAGE

SEASON
- Spring is Storage and Processing
- Summer is Processing
- Fall is Movement
- Winter is Storage

DAY

- Storage goes from 6am to 10am
- Processing goes from 10am to 2pm
- Movement goes from 2pm to 6pm
- Storage goes from 6pm to 10pm
- Processing goes from 10pm to 2am
- Movement goes from 2am to 6am

AGE

- Storage goes from birth to age 16 year old
- Processing goes from 16year old to approximately 50 years
- Movement goes from 50 years through old age

Even though we are simplifying the science, we do need to recognize when the season, day or age matches your dominant energy force because these throw the force off balance. You must then make adjustments to return your body to a healthy balance.

To give an example: You are 58 years old and your main energy force is primarily MOVEMENT. Already you are beginning to notice that your internal balance is more difficult to maintain. The clicking of your joints is increasing. Your mind is very active and you are prone to worry. These problems are not major and can usually be corrected through adjusting your eating habits and practicing gentle exercise such as yoga. Usually, adhering to this routine lets you deviate occasionally without running into difficulties. However, combining minor digressions with a desire for a short run on a cold, windy day may bring a surprise. You begin talking faster. You forget easily and you know it is not early Alzheimers! You begin worrying more and your knees start to bother you.

If we use the same example with a few adjustments, you will see the difference. Your energy force is primarily PROCESSING. The age stays the same. Your eating and daily routines fit your energy profile. You have no clicking of joints. You can go for a short runs on the same cold, windy day with no appreciable effect. WHY? The age is managed by the MOVEMENT energy force, and you have dominant PROCESSING energy force. Cold and wind don't bother you. Running is beneficial for you. This age, or the cold temperature or winds do not have the same affect on a body with a PROCESSING energy force as with someone with a MOVEMENT energy force. If your body does go off balance and MOVEMENT energy increases, then you would see the effects. If we changed the age to 45 years and made it summer time, you would see an effect.

Matching the forces to five elements, recognized in so many cultures, makes it easier for some to comprehend. Studying Ayurveda in depth requires this knowledge. For the layperson, though, the only requisite information is that each force is linked to two elements. This is useful for identifying foods and health conditions. Each of these is an opposing element, balancing each force or energy. Here we are using the Sanskrit terms.

VATA is Air and Ether. Air is like the wind, blowing things as it moves and Ether is a spacey passageway.

PITTA is Fire and Water. Fire consumes or processes and Water puts it out.

KAPHA is Water and Earth. The Earth is solid, stationary and full of nutrients while the Water breaks it down when too much gathers in one place.

Since *Vata* is the force responsible for all movement, or *kinetic* activity in the body, we're calling it the **MOVEMENT ENERGY FORCE.** It is responsible for the movement of food through our digestive system. It is responsible for the movement of thoughts and nerve impulses. It is air and ether and movement is airy and light. It affects our joints and nervous conditions (physical movement plus nerve impulse movement).

Since *Pitta* is the force responsible for balancing and processing, we're calling it the **PROCESSING ENERGY FORCE.** It is responsible for the digestion of our food and the "cooking" of our thoughts. It is fire and water. Somehow this forces or energy knows that how much to process in order to maintain the necessary balance. We can blame it when we begin to gather too many junky or irrelevant details in our minds! It first affects the enzymatic and endocrine systems.

Kapha gets to decide what details or nutrients are important. It provides the stability of the body, surplus or shortage. We're calling it the **STORAGE ENERGY FORCE.** This is also linked to Earth and Water. When there is too much of one thing, the stability is affected; too much is stored just as the Earth builds up. If there is too little, it flows away, like the water.

The following shows the element, the characteristics and the force:

Element	*Characteristics*	*Energy Force*
Earth	Solid and Stable	**STORAGE**

Water	Liquid, continuously moving	
Water	Continuously moving	**PROCESSING**
Fire	Transformation	
Air	Gaseous Mobility	**MOVEMENT**
Ether	No physical Existence, separating Space fields	

As mentioned earlier, everyone already has all three forces, but it is unusual for someone to have them in equal proportions. There are usually two forces more prevalent, with one of them being greater than the other. This makes up seven categories. To illustrate, a person may be:

More MOVEMENT than PROCESSING
More PROCESSING than MOVEMENT
More MOVEMENT than STORAGE
More STORAGE than MOVEMENT
More PROCESSING than STORAGE
More STORAGE than PROCESSING
All equal

Each Force provides us with physical attributes and mental characteristics. We must remember all traits are necessary and none are more desirable than any other, although we might perceive differently. It is also important to remember that while your major force is the one likely to tip out of kilter, the other two are also vulnerable. When one force is more dominant in a person, the following is what you might see.

The Three Energy Forces

MOVEMENT

This force is governed by *kinetic* energy. Its prime characteristics are *changeability, unpredictability and variability!* MOVEMENT - dominant people make active use of energy, spending it freely and wasting energy. This energy or force activates the physical system and allows the body to breathe and circulate blood. This also controls the nervous system.

STORAGE

The **STORAGE** force is governed by potential energy, combining water and earth. Its prime characteristic is relaxed! It forms the body's structure and keeps it 'glued' together. These people tend to store energy, gluing it where needed (or not needed!). This energy becomes the structure of bones, muscle and fat that holds the body together, offering nourishment and protection (immunity). Another way of putting it is - once the body has absorbed food, or an idea, and processed it into useable format, the STORAGE function decides where it should go - cellular storage, excess weight or rejected completely. The STORAGE function also controls the function of mucous membranes.

PROCESSING

The **PROCESSING** force is the *manager* of energy usage. Its prime characteristics are *organized* and *predictable!* It ensures all energy is used efficiently. This function is responsible for the metabolism (fire), processing of food and ideas, and charging the enzymatic activities in the body. It is fire that controls metabolism and digestion. It is also the acid or water that puts it out.

The chart on Page 27 expands these descriptions and gives more details.

Approach to Dis - Ease

Ayurveda practitioners do not label a *dis* - ease or illness. For them, there is only an *im*balance of a particular energy force. For example: A person complained of poor vision and glaucoma was detected. An inexperienced person my immediately assume that it is a PROCESSING forces imbalance since this force governs the eyes. However, glaucoma indicates a STORAGE force *imbalance*. Therefore, diet and herbs could be effective to realign this energy force. Knowing the prime *homes*, the practitioner would look first at the PROCESSING energy, then at the others. It is quite possible that this person also displayed other signs of STORAGE imbalance. Even though the three forces may become imbalanced anywhere, checking out *home* is the first step. These *homes* are:

MOVEMENT:
Large intestine, pelvic cavity, bones, skin, ears and thighs

PROCESSING:
Small intestines, stomach, sweat glands, blood, skin and eyes

STORAGE:
Chest, lungs, spinal fluid and lymph nodes

Initially, when there is an accumulation or excess of one force, it can be corrected through diet and meditation. This is not always evident to the average person. But, once you understand your unique blend of energy forces, imbalances are spotted quite effortlessly. For example, stress tips our internal balance easily. We can then adjust our lifestyle to reduce the stress.

Although Ayurveda does not label, we in the Western world need the security of a name. Here are samples of the ailments are associated with energy imbalances. These lists include both dis - eases that are easily corrected and others that require intervention.

Illnesses Connected With Each Energy Force

MOVEMENT	PROCESSING	STORAGE
Anxiety	Acne	Angina
Arthritis (joints cracking and popping)	Anger (stiffness, swelling)	Arthritis
Brittle nails	Arthritis - inflammation	Asthma
Constipation	Baldness	Cataracts
Dandruff	Thin blood (slow clotting)	Cholesterol
Dry cough	Conjunctivitis	Mucous cough
Earache	Diarrhea	Diabetes
Gas and Flatulence	Gum disease, - bleeding, gingivitis	Fibrocystic Breast Disease
Gum disease - receding	Heartburn	Gallstones
Hemorrhoids	Hemorrhoids	Obesity
Insomnia	Oral Herpes	Sleep apnea
Osteoporosis	Kidney stones	
	Skin rashes and hives	
	Ulcers	

III. KEY POINTS OF ENERGY FORCES

Traits and Ailments of the Three Energy Forces

Movement	Processing	Storage
Thin	Medium build	Heavyset
Prominent Features, joints	Fair, thin hair	Thick, wavy hair
Cool, dry skin	Warm, ruddy, perspiring skin	Cool, thick, pale skin
Hyperactive	Orderly, efficient	Slow, graceful
Moody	Intense	Relaxed
Vivacious	Short temper	Slow to anger
Eats and sleeps at all hours	Lives by the clock	Sleeps long and heavy
Imaginative	Quick intelligence	Affectionate
Nervous disorders	Ulcers, heartburn	Obesity
Constipation	Hemorrhoids	Allergies, sinus
Enthusiastic, infectious and impulsive energy	Passionate tolerant	Forgiving and
Intuitive	Articulate	Compassionate
Cramps	Acne	High cholesterol
Anxiety	Perfectionism	Procrastination
Grasps ideas quickly	Obstinate	

IV. IDENTIFYING YOUR DOMINANT FUNCTIONS

The trained Ayurvedic doctor uses several methods to identify the energy forces within a person. Some are visual and some are tactile. These include: questionnaire, pulse, tongue, facial structure, lips, nails and eyes. Since this is an introductory book, apart from the questionnaire, the descriptions of the techniques are brief. If the reader wants more detail, I recommend the books listed in the bibliography.

It is important to remember that these descriptions are relative. For example, if your family is generally short and robust, you need to look at *your* height compared to this, not at a typical Harlem Globetrotter!

ANALYSIS THROUGH SPECIFIC POINTS

Pulse

Place your first three fingers, index, middle and ring finger over the pulse point with the index finger closest to the wrist. Depending on the energy force of the individual, the strength of the beat will vary amongst the fingers. *MOVEMENT* – dominant people have stronger throbbing under the index finger. The pulse moves smoothly, quickly, evenly, similar to a snake's slithering. *PROCESSING* will have stronger throbbing under the middle finger. The overall movement can be compared to a frog, jumpy and active. *STORAGE* - dominant people will have stronger throbbing under the ring finger. The overall movement is slow, thick and can be compared to a floating swan.

Tongue

The tongue is an excellent indicator of your health, but first you need to identify the base. Generally, the tongue should be pink, clear, and with a bit of a luster. *MOVEMENT* – dominant people have thin and very pointed tongues, possibly able to touch their nose! *PROCESSING* – dominant people have a tongue of medium thickness with a softly pointed tip. A *STORAGE* – *dominant* person has a tongue that is thick and wide.

Face

MOVEMENT - dominant people tend to have sallow skin, sunken cheeks with a crooked - nose shape. *PROCESSING* – dominant people will have a ruddy complexion with a sharp – nose shape.

STORAGE - dominant people, in my opinion, have the most beautiful skin - soft, creamy/oily, and plump cheeks with a blunt nose.

Lips

Again, the *MOVEMENT* - dominant person will have narrow, dry lips. The *STORAGE* person has thick, full, moist lips. The PROCESSING person has naturally redder lips.

Nails

MOVEMENT - *dominant* nails tend to be brittle. PROCESSING – dominant nails are soft, pink and tender. *STORAGE* – *dominant* nails are thick and oily.

Eyes

MOVEMENT – *dominant* eyes are small, nervous with scanty eyelashes. Their irises, are dark, contrasting with muddy –coloured whites. *PROCESSING* – *dominant* eyes are sharp and lustrous. They also have scanty eyelashes with a reddish or yellowish tinge to the iris. *STORAGE* – *dominant* eyes are large, moist with long, thick lashes. The whites of the eyes are very white.

OBSERVATION

The next step is to look closely at the person. There are three ways to gather the information. One of the easiest ways to identify the dominant force is through simple observation. Again, remember the family background and your age or the person being evaluated. Either looking at yourself in a mirror or looking at another person, what do you see?

- Are they thin or tall?
- What is the colour of their hair – light brown, reddish, black or brown?
- Did they turn gray early?
- Taking the age into consideration, is the skin dry and rough or soft and moist?
- Is the skin tone pale or reddish?
- Do they talk fast or is their speech, slow and organized?

INQUIRY:

The next step is to *ask* a few verbal questions. Ask yourself or the other person these six questions:

- Do you have a vigorous appetite or do you pick at food?
- Do you have difficulty digesting your food? Is your stomach sensitive?
- Do you sleep at all hours or do you go to bed and get up a regular time?
- Do you sleep soundly or do you toss and turn?
- Are you always busy, planning in your head or keeping busy with your hands?

- Do you have a good memory, both long and short term?

The last step is to complete a written questionnaire. This takes a little more time because you need to compare yourself to your family, and not the general population. Dark or light, short or tall are relative descriptions. As you go through the questions, you will probably think to yourself: "Well, I am sort of like that, but it's not completely accurate." This is because very few people in this world fit any one picture completely. The descriptions are the extreme ends of spectrum and you are searching for the one that *most sounds like you.*

You also need to consider each question from two perspectives. The first way is going back into your memory of your childhood. This give you a better picture of what your innate constitution should be. The second way is evaluating yourself as you are today. This provides a picture of how you matured plus any probable *im* – balances.

WRITTEN DESCRIPTIONS

Note: Circle the description that best describes that characteristic. It is possible that you fit into more than one area. Mark all and indicate frequency.

1. My overall body build is:
   a. Thin
   b. Moderate
   c. Heavy

2. Generally, I tend to be:
   a. Underweight
   b. Average
   c. Overweight

3. My bone structure is:
   a. Small
   b. Average
   c. Large

4. My skin is:
   a. Dry, rough, cool
   b. Soft, oily, warm, fair
   c. Thick, oily, cool, pale

5. People looking at my hair would best describe it as:
   a. Medium coarseness and light brown or blonde
   b. Very fine hair, soft and oily. It has a reddish tone with eraly gray appearing
   c. Dark brown or black, thick and often wavy

6. My teeth are :
    a. Protruding, big, crooked with emaciated gums.
    b. Moderate in size, yellowish in colour with soft gums.
    c. Strong and white with healthy gums.

7. My eyes are:
    a. Small, dull and dry looking
    b. Sharp and piercing, green or gray in colour
    c. Big, attractive, with thick eyelashes

8. Generally, my appetite is:
    a. Variable, usually sparse
    b. Good, excessive, needs regular meals
    c. Slow and steady, favorite pastime

9. My favorite meals are:
    a. Warm and moist or oily
    b. Cold
    c. Warm and dry

10. My preferred food tastes are:
    a. Sweet, sour and salty
    b. Sweet, bitter or astringent
    c. Pungent, bitter or astringent

11. I would describe my fluid consumption as:
    a. Variable
    b. Too much
    c. Scanty

12. My first choice for climate is:
    a. Moderate, dislike for the cold
    b. Cool or temperate; I perspire easily
    c. Dry and warm; I do tolerate extremes

13. My bowel movements are:
    a. Dry, hard, with frequent constipation
    b. Soft, oily, loose
    c. Thick, oily, heavy, slow

14. Generally, I am:
    a. Very active
    b. Moderate
    c. Lethargic

15. My energy level:
    a. Fluctuates, comes in waves
    b. Is moderate to high. I tend to push myself too hard
    c. Is steady

16. My mental activity is:
    a. Restless, busy
    b. Aggressive and Intelligent
    c. Calm and slow

17. Words that describe my emotional temperament are:
    a. Fearful, insecure, unpredictable
    b. Aggressive, irritable, jealous
    c. Calm, greedy, attached, clinging

18. My faith is:
    a. Changeable
    b. Fanatic
    c. Steady

19. My memory is:
    a. Short-term Memory is good, but I forget easily
    b. Sharp
    c. Slow, but prolonged

20. When I dream, the theme is usually:
    a. Fearful, flying, jumping, running
    b. Fiery, anger, violence, war
    c. Watery, river, ocean, swimming

21. My sleep pattern is:
    a. Scanty, with frequent interruptions
    b. Little, but sound
    c. Heavy and long

22. My speaking is:
    a. Fast
    b. Sharp and cutting
    c. Slow, monotonous

23. My pulse is:
    a. Thin, weak and moves like a snake
    b. Moderate and broad, jumps like a frog
    c. Slow and moves like a swan

24. My attitude to money is:
    a.   Poor. I spend money quickly on trifles
    b.   Moderate. I love spending on luxuries
    c.   Good. I'm a money-saver, unless its spending on food

In all the choices above, "**a**" describes the traits of someone with a dominance of MOVEMENT energy. "**b**" gives the characteristics of someone with a dominance of **PROCESSING** energy. Finally, all the "c" choices describe someone with **STORAGE** energy.

Recognizing Minor Imbalances

I want to stress the word minor. When you suspect any major change in your body, it is imperative to consult a health practitioner. Whether you choose a Medical doctor, Ayurvedic physician, Naturopath or other alternative practitioner is up to you. However, there are many indicators of an *im*balance within your body that could lead to *dis*-ease. These can be reversed through diet and lifestyle changes.

Eyes

Our eyes tell a great deal about our health. The following are the general indications of the healthy *energy functions.* Some imbalances can also be spotted by a novice. Again, I stress that only a slight tipping of the equilibrium can be corrected without a trained practitioner.

Evidence of Balanced, Healthy Eyes

- **MOVEMENT – dominant:** Small, nervous, dry, scanty lashes. Whites are muddy, while iris is dark
- **PROCESSING – dominant:** Moderate, sharp, lustrous and sensitive to light. Lashes are scanty and oily while iris is red or yellowish
- **STORAGE – dominant:** Large, moist with long, thick lashes. Whites are very white while iris is pale

Imbalance Indication and Possible Causes

Symptom	Cause
Prominent eyes	Thyroid dysfunction
Conjunctiva is pale	Weak Liver
Small iris	Weak joints
White ring around the iris	Excessive intake of salt or sugar
Brownish – black spots in the iris	Unabsorbed iron in the intestine

Nails

Nails are the waste products of your bones. They will tell you whether nutrients are being absorbed efficiently or if there is a chronic, on – going condition.

Understanding the condition of our nails helps us understand the condition of our health.

Signs of Balanced Energy on the Finger Nails

Healthy, ideal nails will have these traits:

- **MOVEMENT** – the prevailing energy is shown through brittle nails.
- **PROCESSING** – energy produces soft, pink and tender nails.
- **STORAGE** – prevailing energy produces thick, strong and oily nails.

Imbalance Indication and Possible Causes

- Longitudinal lines   Mal – absorption of nutrients
- Blue nails   Delicate lungs and heart
- Concave   Iron deficiency
- White spots   Zinc or calcium Deficiency
- Pale nails   Possible Anemia
- Convex and Bulbous   Lungs or heart problems

V. GENERAL HEALTH IMBALANCES AND MAINTENANCE

The observable imbalances listed above do help identify the need for changes in habits. However, it is more usual to see a change in mental or personal behavior. Knowing who we are and using the charts below allows us to do random checks on ourselves and *catch* the times when we feel disconnected. The following charts are divided by energy forces. Remember, though, that we are subject to imbalances in ANY energy force, not just our dominant one.

Symptoms of MOVEMENT Imbalance

For a person with a dominant MOVEMENT energy force, *the imbalance indicators are:*

Mental	Behavioral	Physical
Worry, anxiety	Insomnia	Constipation
Overactive mind	Fatigue	Dry or rough skin
Impatience	Inability to relax	Low stamina, loss of energy
Loss of focus	Restlessness	Chapped skin, lips
Short attention span	Low appetite flatulence	Intestinal gas,
Depression, psychosis	Impulsiveness	Lower back pain
	Agitation Joints	Aching or arthritic
	Weight loss, Emaciated tissue	
	Muscle spasms	
	Or Numbness	
	Acute pain	

Ways to Correct or Maintain

How to maintain status quo

- Regular routine
- Stay warm
- Quiet
- Get plenty of fluids
- Steady supply of nourishment
- Decrease sensitivity to stress
- Ample rest
- Regular massage

Simple correction techniques

- Get plenty of rest; rest for 5 minutes during any activity
- Stay warm with adequate humidity in the rooms
- Avoid drafts
- Eat a MOVEMENT – pacifying diet: Sweet, Sour and Salty foods
- Eat regular meals: at least three or more smaller meals
- Drink LOTS of warm fluids
- Massage your body every morning with sesame oil
- Avoid mental strain and over – stimulating yourself, such as with loud music and violent TV

Symptoms of PROCESSING Imbalance

For a person with a dominant PROCESSING energy force, the imbalance indicators are:

Mental	Behavioral	Physical
Anger	Outbursts of temper boils, rashes	Skin inflammations,
Self – criticism	Argumentative Stance	Excessive hunger or thirst
Irritability, impatience	Tyrannical behavior	Bad breath and sour body orders of
Resentment	Criticism of others	Ulcers
	Intolerance of delays	Heartburn, acid stomach

Ways to Correct or Maintain

How to maintain status quo

- Do everything in moderation
- Avoid high temperatures
- Attention to leisure
- Spend time outdoors in nature
- Balance of rest and activity
- Decrease stimulants

Simple correction techniques

- Take time to wind down, alternate rest and activity
- Don't linger in hot baths, keep room temp low
- Eat a PROCESSING and pacifying diet: **sweet, astringent and bitter tastes**
- Avoid stimulants
- Eat regularly, small meals

Symptoms of STORAGE Imbalance

For a person with a dominant STORAGE energy force, the imbalance indicators are:

Mental	Behavioral	Physical
Dullness, mental inertia	Procastination of cold and damp	Intolerance
Sluggish, lethargic	Inability to accept change, rigid	Sinus congestion, runny nose
Stupor, depression	Oversleeping, drowsiness	Fluid retention and bloating
Clingy, over attachment	Greed	High cholesterol
	Slow movements	Heaviness in limbs
	Possessiveness	Allergies, asthma
	Cysts and other growths	
	Diabetes	
	Loose, aching joints	

Ways to Correct or Maintain

Maintaining the status quo

- Look for stimulation
- Variety of experiences
- Regular exercise
- Warmth, dryness
- Weight control
- Reduced sweetness

Simple correction techniques

- Seek variety in life
- Eat STORAGE – pacifying diet: pungent, astringent and bitter foods
- Reduce sweetness
- Stay warm
- Avoid dampness
- Perform a DRY massage regularly
- Drink warm fluids during the day
- Exercise regularly, preferably everyday
- Acknowledge illness and go to bed

Regardless of your dominant energy force, the MOVEMENT function is most likely to go out of balance, especially as we get older. Therefore, it becomes very important to stay in balance, particularly when this is your dominant force. In this way disease is caught in the beginning stages. I refer the reader to the section on seasons, time and age. By paying attention to the indications, an individual can begin to identify his/her personal functional imbalances and implement a few actions to bring them back into balance.

> *N.B This assumes that good health normally exists and the imbalance is short term. It also does not preclude regular visits to your health care provider.*

VI. MAINTAINING A BALANCE

General Guidelines to Maintain a Balanced Body and Mind

- **Eat a proper diet** which contains ALL six tastes. This will keep your body balanced according to your internal energy blend.
- **Exercise and yoga** kindles the internal fire, improves circulation, stimulates metabolism and sharpens the mind.
- **Meditation** enhances self – awareness and awareness of one's environment.
- **Herbs,** prescribed by an Ayurvedic Physician, rebuilds and rejuvenates the body.
- **Massage,** using herbal oils, removes toxins from the system
- **Sun** improves circulation, aids absorption of vitamin D and strengthens the bones.
- **Deep Breathing** brings a sense of tranquillity, peace and alleviates stress in our lives.

General Guidelines for Food Choice

Once you have identified the dominant energy force within your body, it needs to be kept at that level for optimum health. The easiest balancer is your diet since all foods can be divided into six tastes. When we incorporate all of these tastes into our diet, your energy forces should not shift. While identifying a taste is not difficult, it does take some practice. For example, an orange is considered sweet even though we may experience a tangy pucker when we eat them. Personally, I find it easier is to look at a list of items and then choosing equally from each list. Analyzing each one takes more time. It is only when your body is tipped off its fulcrum, that you need to place emphasis on a particular list.

- Whenever possible, use fresh and natural produce, free from artificial chemicals.
- Avoid leftovers and all foods that are old.
- Use the best quality food you can afford.
- Favor cooked food (except fruit) over raw, they are easier to digest. Salads can be handled well by the dominant PROCESSING force as they are cooling. Someone with a dominant MOVEMENT energy force should use an oily dressing on their salads.
- Don't heat honey and never bake with it.
- Avoid heavy foods in the evening.
- Avoid ice – cold foods and drinks as they interfere with digestion.
- Fried food is hard for digestive enzymes.

- Lean toward a vegetarian diet. Meats are heavy, hard to digest and putrefy in the digestive tract. The MOVEMENT energy force tolerates meat are more readily because it is grounding.
- Milk should be taken separately from major meals but does not combine well with grains. It is also better for you when it is heated. Improving digestibility can be achieved by added a pinch of turmeric, ginger or cardamom. See below for more information about milk and milk products.
- Wait at least an hour before any strenuous exercise.

"A stroll of 100 steps" help digestion.

Best Time to Eat

These are the guiding principles for each dominant force:

- Those with the prevailing **PROCESSING** force require three regular meals a day and sometimes need snacks in between. They should leave a gap of at least three or four hours in between. Good snacks are sweet fruit and/or dried fruit.
- STORAGE people can get away skipping breakfast. They shouldn't feel they have to eat three meals a day. They tend not to feel hungry but, when out of balance, are the most prone to overeat. They should leave at least six hours between meals.
- MOVEMENT – dominant people MUST eat at regular times. They should respect the variability of their appetite, but eating on schedule is important. Those with this dominant force can lose their appetite quickly if they don't eat when they are hungry or at a set time. It is best to have three or four light meals a day with snacks in between, leaving a gap of at least two hours.
- Avoid rushing your eating. Be relaxed.

How Much

- The objective is to feel satisfied but not stuffed. Eating only 2/3 or ¾ of your capacity achieves this.
- Eat approximately the quantity of food that you could hold by cupping your two hands together.
- Filling your stomach 1/3 with food and 1/3 with liquid leaves 1/3 empty for digestion process.

Enjoy Yourself

- Eat sitting down, in a relaxed setting.
- After sitting down, take a moment to relax and settle into the activity. This aids digestion.
- Pay attention to what you are doing. It will slow you down.

- Avoid distractions such as TV or reading. These tend to divert blood flow from the stomach.
- Chew your food well until it is soft. Putting your fork down between mouthfuls promotes this practice
- Avoid stress or tension during a meal.
- Sit for 5 minutes after a meal before getting up.
- Take a short walk (100 steps).

The following pages are a *guideline* only; your body tolerates almost all foods. However, toleration does not mean something is the best food for you. Craving exist; which is what makes us human. If you want to eat something that is not on a list, give yourself permission. If the item *increases* the *amount* of a force within your body, then enjoy a small quantity. The secret is to be sure to include foods *reducing* the same energy function. For example:

1. Carrots increase the fire of the PROCESSING force. But when you include cucumber and celery in the same meal as they reduce the Fire. You will not see carrots on the list below.
2. *MOVEMENT* – predominant people should not eat cold foods. However, a solution might be eating a salad at the same meal as a warm dish, such as soup.

VII. FOOD GUIDELINES FOR MOVEMENT DOMINANCE

> **The balancing tastes for this energy force is:**
> Sweet, Sour and Salty foods

A dominant MOVEMENT body already has sufficient amounts of cold and dry. Therefore, it is important to consume foods that are moist and warm to balance off what the body already carries. When food is dry, cold and gaseous, this encourages the body to take the moisture and warmth from other parts of the body.

Note: It is important to remember that temperature is not the taste but rather what reaction it has on our internal system. During hot weather we drink hot tea because it has a cooling effect on our internal system.

If a food is not on this list, then

- Avoid it whenever possible, OR
- Eat it partially cooked, OR
- Eat a small quantity with larger amounts of preferred foods.

RECOMMENDED FOODS

Vegetables

Asparagus	Okra (cooked)
Beets	Radishes
Carrots	Sweet potatoes
Cucumber	Turnips
Onions and Garlic	Green Beans
(not raw)	

Fruits

Avocados	Bananas
Apricots	Berries
Figs	Coconut

Dates

Grapes	Cherries
Lemons	Grapefruit
Nectarines	Mango
Oranges	Melons
Pineapple	Papayas
Stewed fruits	Peaches

Sweet, well – ripened fruit in general

Grains

Oats (as cooked, oat – meal cereal, not dry)
Wheat

Dairy

All are fine,
in moderation

Meat

Chicken & Turkey Seafood, in general
(white meat)
(All acceptable,
in small quantities

Oils

Sesame oil is the best   Generally, all
                                oils are Good

Herbs & Spices

Allspice	Anise
Basil	Bay leaf
Caraway	Cardamom
Cilantro (green coriander)	Cinnamon
Clove	Cumin
Fennel	Ginger
Licorice root	Marjoram
Mustard	Nutmeg
Oregano and Sage	Tarragon
Thyme	

Sweeteners

All are acceptable

Nuts and Seeds

Almonds are the best
Choice
Since the MOVEMENT force needs oil, all oils
are acceptable in small quantities

Legumes (Beans)

| Chickpeas | Mung beans |
| Pink Lentils | Tofu (in small amounts) |

Generally legumes are gaseous which aggravates the ether component of the MOVEMENT force

General Guidelines

- Warm food, moderately heavy textures
- Added butter & fat (remember cholesterol levels)
- Soothing and satisfying foods
- No spice should be used in large quantities
- Minimize all bitter and astringent foods

VIII. FOOD GUIDELINES PROCESSING DOMINANCE

> **The balancing tastes for this energy force is:**
> Sweet, Astringent and Bitter Foods

These people already have sufficient fire and moisture in their body to handle the processing. Therefore, they need to eat drier and cooler foods. The astringent and bitter tastes will offset the hot, spicy foods. If the food is NOT on the list, it should be avoided.

RECOMMENDED FOODS

Vegetables (Sweet and bitter vegetables)

Asparagus	Broccoli
Brussels sprouts	Cabbage
Cauliflower	Celery
Cucumber	Green beans
Leafy green vegetables	Lettuce
Mushroom	Okra
Peas	Potatoes, white and
	Sweet
Sprouts	Sweet peppers
Zucchini	

Fruits (All should be sweet and ripe)

Avocados	Coconut
Figs	Grapes
Mangoes	Melons
Oranges	Pears
Pineapple	Plums

Prunes and Raisins
Avoid fruits that come to market sour or unripe
Green grapes, oranges, pineapple and plums
SHOULD BE SWEET

Dairy

Butter (unsalted) or Ghee (clarified butter)

Egg Whites — Ice cream
Milk — Cottage Cheese

Grains

Barley — Oats (cooked)
Wheat — White rice (basmati and white)

Meat (in small quantities)

Chicken — Rabbit
Shrimp — Turkey

Beans

Chickpeas — Mung beans
Tofu and other
soybean products

Sweeteners

All sweeteners okay — Molasses
except Honey

Oils

Coconut, Soy — Olive, Sunflower

Nuts and Seeds

Coconut — Pumpkin and Sunflower seeds

Herbs and Spices

Spices are generally too heating for the body, but some sweet, bitter and astringent ones are okay – in small quantity

Cardamom — Cilantro (green coriander)
Cinnamon — Dill and Fennel
Mint — Saffron and Turmeric

General guidelines – Strive for

Moderately heavy textures	Temperature choice: Cool or warm, not steaming hot foods
Bitter, sweet and astringent tastes	Minimize butter and added fat

IX. FOOD GUIDELINES FOR STORAGE DOMINANCE

The balancing tastes for this energy force is:
Pungent, Astringent and Bitter Foods

STORAGE – dominant people are already moist, heavy and cool. Therefore, they need to eat drier and warmer foods. The hot, spicy foods balance and reduce the cold and dampness; they have sufficient oil in their body already.

RECOMMENDED FOODS

Vegetables

Generally, all vegetables are good	Asparagus
Beets	Broccoli
Brussels Sprouts	Cabbage
Carrots	Cauliflower
Celery	Eggplant
Garlic	Leafy green vegetables
Lettuce	Mushrooms
Okra	Onions
Peas	Peppers
Potatoes	Radishes
Spinach	Sprouts

Fruits

Apples	Apricots
Berries	Cherries
Cranberries	Peaches
Pears	Pomegranates
Generally, all dried fruits is good	

Grains

Barley	Buckwheat
Corn	Millet
Oats (dry)	Rice (basmati, small amount)
Rye	

Dairy

Skim milk and minimum whole milk	Boiled or poached eggs

Oils

Almond	Corn
Safflower	Sunflower

Meat

Chicken	Shrimp
Turkey (all in small amounts)	

Sweeteners

Raw, unheated honey

Nuts and Seeds

Sunflower seeds	Pumpkin seeds

Herbs and Spices

All spices are good	Ginger is best for improving digestion

General Guidelines

Warm, light food	Dry food, cooked without much water
Butter, oil and sugar throw the energy force off	Stimulating foods are good

X. BLENDING EASTERN AND WESTERN DIETS

Thanks to Western science, we' ve learned the body requires individual vitamins and minerals, all essential for health. Each energy force of Ayurveda benefits from different foods for these nutrients. This table shows us which foods are best for each person to get the required nutrition.

Note: Since nutritional charts normally use four character abbreviations, we are doing the same. At the bottom of the following charts, at the end of the chapter, all of the nutrients are decoded.

SEASON

Spring	S P
Summer	P
Fall	M
Winter	S

DAY

6am	S	
10am	2pm	P
2pm	6pm	M
6pm	10pm	S
10pm	2am	P
2am	6am	M

AGE

Birth	6-16 years	S
Adult	16-50	P
Old Age	M	

On the following pages, you will find a series of tables which show us Western Nutritional and Sources in comparison with the Ayurveda – Best sources for each dominant energy.

Western Nutrition and sources		Ayurveda – Best source for each dominant energy		
Nutr	Best Sources	Movement Energy	Processing Energy	Storage Energy
Fiber	*Water Soluble* Barley, Fruits, Legumes, Oats, Rye, Seeds, Vegetables Onion and *Water Insoluble* Brown Rice Vegetables Wheat bran Whole grains	Asparagus Beets Carrots Cucumber Green beans Mangoes Garlic Sweet potatoes Rice Wheat Oats *Avoid* Apples Cranberries Pears Melon Dried fruit	Barley Apples Avocados Coconut Figs Grapes Peaches Melons Oranges Pears Pineapple Plum Chickpeas Mung beans Oats, cooked Coconut Pumpkin seeds Sunflower Wheat	Barley Apples Apricots Berries Cherries Cranberries Pears Dried fruit oats White rice Rye Sunflower seeds Pumpkin seeds *Avoid* Sweet vegetables Cucumber Tomatoes Sweet Potatoes
Carb	Vegetable Milk Fruit Breads	Vegetables Fruits Grains Milk in moderation	Sweet & bitter vegetables Asparagus Broccoli Brussels sprouts Cabbage Cauliflower Celery Cucumber Greenbeans	Vegetables Skim Milk Fruit Rye bread

			Potatoes, sweet and white Fruit Grains	
Fats	Plain potatoes Nonfat milk Fish, seafood Leafy vegetable Seeds Nuts Grains beans All oils (Sesame Oil is best)	Chicken & Turkey Seafood Almonds Asparagus Green Leafy vegetable Coconut Pumpkin seeds Sunflower seeds **no seafood**	Coconut Olive Soy oil Sunflower Baked potatoes	Almond oil Corn oil Safflower oil Sunflower oil **Little oil as possible**
Prot.	Lean meat, fish Shellfish, Eggs Low fat Nonfat Milk Yogurt Cheese Dry beans and peas, cooked Leafy greens Nuts Grains	Chicken & Turkey Seafood All dairy products in moderation Chickpeas Mung beans Pink lentils Tofu All nuts Grains - oats, wheat	White meat Seafood Milk Chickpeas Mung beans Leafy greens Nuts Barley oats, cooked Wheat White rice	Chicken Shrimp Turkey Eggs Low fat milk Leafy greens Sunflower seeds Pumpkin seeds **Avoid** Kidney beans Soy beans Black lentils Mung beans
VT-A	Fortified milk Sweet potato Carrots Apricots Spinach	Milk Sweet potatoes Carrots Apricots	Milk Sweet potatoes	Skim milk Carrots Apricots Spinach
VT-D	Sunlight	Sunlight	Egg whites	Eggs

	Eggs Fortified milk Shrimp Margarine	Eggs Milk Shrimp	Milk Clarified butter	Skim milk
VT-E	Corn oil Safflower oil Sunflower seeds Canola oil Sweet potato Shrimp	All oils Sweet potatoes Shrimp	Coconut oil Olive oil Soy Sunflower oil Sweet potatoes	Almond oil Corn oil Safflower oil Sunflower oil
VT-K	Cabbage Spinach Cauliflower Milk Eggs Garbanzo beans Beef liver	Milk Eggs Garbanzo beans Chickpeas	Cabbage Cauliflower Milk Egg whites Garbanzo	Cabbage Spinach Skim milk Eggs beans
Thia	Green peas Pork chops Black beans Melon Whole wheat bread Sunflower seeds	Black beans Wheat Seeds	Peas Black beans Melon Whole wheat bread Sunflower seeds	Peas Black beans Melon Sunflower seeds
Ribo	Milk Cottage cheese Yogurt Spinach Beef liver	Milk Cottage cheese Beef liver	Milk Mushroom	Skim milk Spinach Mushrooms
Niac	Baked potato Mushroom Tuna Chicken breast Pork chop	Tuna Chicken breast	Baked potato Mushrooms Chicken breast	Baked potatoes Mushrooms Chicken breast
Fola	Liver Asparagus Spinach	Beef Liver Asparagus cantaloupe	Asparagus Melon Pinto beans	Asparagus Spinach Melon

	Cantaloupe Pinto beans Beets	Pinto beans Beets	Beets Beets	Pinto Beans
VT=B6	Baked poatato Beef liver Banana	Beef liver Bananas (ripe)	Baked potato	Baked potato
VT=B12	Cottage cheese Beef Tuna Chicken liver Sardines Sardines foods	Cottage cheese Tuna Chicken Liver Supplemented	Tuna Chicken Liver Sardines Eggs	Chicken and turkey (large quantities) Milk
Biot	Eggs	Eggs	Egg white	Eggs
Panto	Milk Whole wheat bread Broccoli Chicken breast Pinto beans Beef liver	Milk Wheat Chicken breast Pinto beans Liver	Milk Wheat Broccoli Chicken breast Pinto beans	Broccoli Chicken breast Pinto beans
VT-C	Broccoli Sweet red pepper Berries Grapefruit Orange juice Brussels sprouts Green pepper	Berries Grapefruit Orange juice sprouts	Broccoli Sweet peppers Brussels sprouts Green peppers	Broccoli Peppers Berries Brussels
Calc	Milk Pork and beans Cheddar cheese Greens Almonds	Milk Beans (no pork) Cheddar cheese Almonds	Milk Greens Almonds	Low fat milk Greens

Phos	Milk Cottage cheese Navy beans Sirloin steak Salmon All animal tissues	Milk Cottage cheese Navy beans Salmon Chicken & turkey	Milk Navy beans Salmon Chicken Turkey Rabbit	Low fat milk Navy beans Chicken Turkey
Magn	Nuts Oysters Dried fig Black–eyed peas Dark green vegetables (spinach) Baked potato Sunflower seeds Chocolate and cocoa	Almonds Sunflower seeds Chocolate	Coconut Dark green vegetables Baked potato Black-eyed peas Sunflower seeds	Dried figs Dark green vegetables Baked potato Sunflower seeds Pumpkin seeds
Pota	Whole foods Milk baked fish Raisins Cantaloupe Baked potato Banana Lima beans	Milk Baked fish cantaloupe Ripe bananas	Milk Raisins Melon Baked potato	Low fat milk Baked fish Raisins Baked potato
Sodi	Salt, soy sauce, processed foods	Salt, little Soy sauce		
Iron	Swiss chard Clams Sirloin steak Tofu Navy beans Dried fruits	Clams Tofu (in small quantities Navy beans	Swiss chard Tofu	Swiss chard Tofu Navy beans Dried fruit
Iodi	Seafood Iodized salt (**not sea salt!**)	Seafood Salt Milk	Milk Low fat milk	Shrimp

Milk

Zinc	Black beans Crabmeat Yogurt Green peas Oysters Sirloin steak	Black beans Crabmeat Yogurt	Black beans Green peas	Black beans Green peas
Sele	Seafood Organ meats Most vegetables	Seafood Asparagus Beets Carrots Cucumber Green beans Sweet potatoes	Chicken liver Vegetables, as above	Shrimp Vegetables above

*Biot=Biotin	Calc=Calcium
Carb=Carbohydrate	Fola=Folate
Iodi=Iodine	Magn=Magnesium
Niac=Niacin	Panto=Pantotheic Acid
Phos=Phosphorous	Pota=Potassium
Prot=Protein	Ribo=Riboflavin
Sele=Selenium	Sodi=Sodium
Thia=Thiamin	VT=Vitamins

XI. FOOD COMPATIBILITY

The premise behind various health systems is that certain foods must be consumed with other foods and some combinations should be avoided. Ayurveda is no exception. Incorrect consumption leads to poor digestion and nutrient absorption. Many of the don'ts from ancient practices have also been identified in this century by Western scientists. The following is a brief summary of combinations to avoid–

- Avoid taking foods that have an opposing reaction in the body at the same meal. Examples are milk and fish or bananas and milk.
- Avoid eating dairy products with sour foods or yeast products at the same meal. For example, lemons don't mix with yogurt or milk.
- Melons should always be eaten alone. Especially avoid eating them with fried foods or grain products such as bread or oatmeal.
- Most fruits are best eaten *before* a meal since their enzymes assist digestion.
- Avoid having any two concentrated proteins at one meal. One example is our traditional pork and beans.
- Eggs do not go well with milk or cheese, fruit or potatoes. There goes the cheese omelette with hash brown.
- Heavy starches do not go well with bananas and dates.
- Never heat or cook honey and avoid combining it with butter and grains.
- Nightshade foods are not handled well by the body. If you must have nightshades, do not have them with dairy products or cucumber. They are particularly disturbing to those with a dominant MOVEMENT energy force. Nightshade foods are white potatoes, tomatoes, eggplant and green peppers.

XII. SPECIFIC FOOD PRODUCT INFORMATION

While some foods are included in a specific category, we need additional information. A product might be useful for all energy forces but the preparation will vary. Also, knowing how they work in either the stomach or in combination with other foods is useful for maintaining a healthy internal energetic balance.

Dairy

- Milk is heavy and has a cold action in the stomach.
- Pacifies the MOVEMENT and PROCESSING forces but will increase the STORAGE force.
- Adding spices that compliment each Energy force is good. Ginger, cardamom and saffron are good in milk.

Cow's Milk as pure as possible – no chemicals

- Sweet, cool energy
- Life – giving
- Increases intelligence and memory power
- Laxative
- Good for urinary diseases and bleeding

Goat's Milk

- Satisfies Sweet, Astringent and Salty tastes
- Very light, easy to digest
- Not as nourishing as cow's milk
- Good for fever, asthma, tuberculosis, diarrhea and digestion

Yogurt

- Combining ice or sour fruit with yogurt is not good.
- Combining sour fruit and milk is not recommended.
- Yogurt is hot to the body and heavy to digest.
- Causes constipation.

- Increases STORAGE and PROCESSING forces, calms the MOVEMENT force.
- Good as an appetizer since it increases digestive fire.
- In excess it can cause fattening increases the STOARGE within the body, water retention, excess menstrual bleeding, skin diseases, anemia, high blood pressure.
- Is good if taken with honey, mung beans, ghee, and sugar.
- It is best taken early in the day, not the evening. Not recommended for daily consumption.

Buttermilk

- Adding Acidophilus to yogurt is approximately equal to buttermilk.
- It is both astringent and sour in taste. This makes it acceptable for all three energy forces. MOVEMENT – Sweet, *Sour* and Salty. PROCESSING – Sweet, *Astringent* and Bitter. However, the quantity will affect energy.
- Pacifies STORAGE and MOVEMENT functions and will increase the PROCESSING energy.
- Reduces cholesterol.

Butter

- Butter reduces the MOVEMENT and PROCESSING forces while increasing the STORAGE energy.
- Sweet and Astringent taste.
- Increases the colour of the skin, body, strength and digestive power.
- When consumed in excess, it causes constipation.
- Good remedy when vomiting blood, for tuberculosis, haemorrhoids, eye diseases and vocal cords.

Clarified Butter or GHEE

- Calms all the functioning energies, especially the PROCESSING force within the body.
- Sweet – tasting, cold digesting action.
- Good for intelligence, memory power, understanding, mental discrimination.
- It is an excellent remedy for the eyes providing you can get PURE clarified butter and it I applied externally.
- Good for mental diseases and stomach ulcers.
- While not as harmful for those with high cholesterol as butter or margarine, caution should still be taken.

Sugars

Cane Sugar

- In small quantities, it reduces the PROCESSING and MOVEMENT forces but increases the STORAGE force within.
- Increases energy.
- Acts as an aphrodisiac.
- Reduces bleeding
- Should be used moderately.

Black Molasses

- Difficult to digest.
- Mild Laxative.
- Good for kidney disorders and purification of urine

*Jaggery (*Indian lump sugar made from molasses)

- Increases the STORAGE function.
- Helps to remove constipation.
- In excess, reduces digestive fire.

Honey

- Reduces STORAGE function and fat when taken in moderation.
- Sweet and Astringent taste.
- Revitalizing.
- Good for the eyes, skin diseases, asthma, cough, dysentery.
- Cleanses ulcers, helps healing and mending together wounds.
- Wild honey can be taken by diabetics.
- Honey and Ghee in equal quantities is toxic.

AVOID

- Cooking alters honey's attributes and it becomes incompatible with the body.

Maple Syrup

- Reduces the MOVEMENT and PROCESSING energies, increases STORAGE.
- Revitalizes the body.
- A mild aphrodisiac.

Oils

Sesame Oil

- Pacifies all energy forces but is best for the MOVEMENT force
- Sweet and Astringent
- Hot digestive fire
- Good for skin, eyes, hair
- Reduces worms
- It is the best base for herbs

Mustard Oil

- Reduces STORAGE and MOVEMENT energies. Increases PROCESSING force.
- Pungent taste, hot digestive fire.
- Reduces worms and parasites.
- Helps to protect the body from cold weather.
- Can burn when heated. Don't use on sensitive skin.
- Black mustard seed is best type of mustard seed.

Castor Oil

- Reduces MOVEMENT energy as well as STORAGE energy.
- Sweet, bitter and pungent taste, heavy and hot digestive fire.
- Laxative.
- Good for swelling, back pain, arthritis (internal and external)
- Will reduce fibroids through massage.

Wheat

- Pacifies all three functioning energies.
- Tonic for all parts of the body.
- *In excess*, can increase the STORAGE energy, and body fat.
- Increases body strength and semen.

Rice

- Little bulk with rice.
- Brown rice is not good for weak digestion.
- Pacifies all the functioning energies but in excess will increase MOVEMENT and STORAGE energy forces.

- Nourishing for all parts of the body.
- Increases body strength and semen.
- *In excess*, causes constipation and scanty stool.

XIII. REMEDIES

In the Western world, we are very quick to go to our pharmacist and our physician for a pill solution. There are, however, many ways that we can correct the imbalance ourselves. The first step is to look at the foods we are eating. Once we identify the energy force that is tilted, then we can slightly increase the amount of foods from that particular list. It is important to remember that we need to return to a regular diet as soon as we can. For specific ailments, there are other solutions to make us feel better. Here are a few remedies to common ailments:

Depression

Depression is caused by excess MOVEMENT energy in the body.

1. Eat foods that strengthen; whole grains, vegetables cooked in oil.
2. Regulate routine and early bedtime.
3. Daily self massage with sesame oil.
4. Keep warm, avoid drafts.
5. Mild exercise such as walking.
6. Daily meditation at a regular time.
7. Relaxing music.
8. Herbs: anise, cinnamon, cumin, ginger, gotu kola, licorice, nutmeg, sesame seed and valerian.

Anger

Anger is caused by too much fire (PROCESSING) energy.

1. Soothing music.
2. Daily self – massage.
3. Nose drops (liquefied ghee).
4. Eat a Fire – pacifying diet, mostly salads and vegetables. Avoid onion, garlic, and sweet fruit.
5. Follow natural rhythms, physical heat caused internal heat – anger.
6. Keep order and beauty in your life.
7. Follow a regular routine.
8. Meditate regularly.
9. Herbs: cilantro, licorice, coriander, fennel, mint, gotu kola.
10. Practice yoga and love.

Cankers

I think everyone at some time of their life has been bothered by cankers. There are two ways to treat these bothersome creatures, one internal and one topical.

Internally, this is a high PROCESSING energy affliction. While it doesn't bring relief, the first thing to do is switch to a PROCESSING diet. Drinking ½ cup of PURE cranberry juice in between meals relieves the burning and irritation.

Topical remedies include:

- Rinsing your mouth several times a day with aloe vera juice.
- Making a mouth rinse of 10 drops of tea tree oil in 1/3 cup of water. Rinse frequently.
- While it doesn't taste very good, applying tea tree oil directly onto the canker sore speeds healing.

Congestion and Mucous Coughs

Gargling mixture

- Use Hot water and Salt.
- Chamomile Tea – wait for it to cool. Note: *Do not use with dry cough.*

Teas and drinks

- Hot tea
- Freshly pressed orange juice
- Hot lemon
- Recipe #1:
  => 11 leaves of fresh basil (or *1 tsp. of dried leaves*)
  => 2 grams fresh ginger (¼ tsp. dried)
  => 5 black pepper grains
  => Crush together and add to 1 cup boiling water
  => Cook covered over low heat. Filter and add pinch of sugar.
  => After drinking, lie down under blanket and sweat. Do this 2-3 times a day.
- Recipe #2:
  => Cook 1 ½ tablespoon of dried chickpea flour in 1 tsp. of ghee (clarified butter) on a low fire.
  => When it is cooked, add a glass of water, stirring constantly.
  => Add 2-3 tsp. sugar and continue stirring. Bring to a boil and cook for another 30 seconds.
  => Lie down after drinking. Cover yourself well. Take 2-3 times a day.

Throat Lozenges

- Recipe #1:
  Suggestion: Make a large quantity and include them in gift packages.
  => Ingredients:
  - => 1 tsp. cardamom
  - => 1 tsp Laurel leaves
  - => 1 tsp Cinnamon
  - => pinch black pepper
  - => 2 tbs. of dried dates
  - => 2 tbs. of dried raisins
  - => 2 tbs. licorice.

  => With a mortar and pestle crush everything except dates and raisins into a powder. Press this through a cloth to make a fine powder. Crush dates and raisins and mix with powder to form a fine paste. Add honey to make a thick paste.
  => Roll in your palm to make small lozenges. Dry in the shade.
  => Will calm down cough and clear voice.

- Recipe #2:
  => Cook 1 ½ tablespoon of dried chickpea flour in 1 tsp. of ghee (clarified butter) on a low fire.
  => When it is cooked, add a glass of water, stirring constantly.
  => Add 2-3 tsp. sugar and continue stirring. Bring to a boil and cook for another 30 seconds.
  => Lie down after drinking. Cover yourself well. Take 2-3 times a day.

Throat Lozenges

- Recipe #1:
  Suggestion: Make a large quantity and include them in gift packages.
  => Ingredients:
  - => 1 tsp. cardamom
  - => 1 tsp Laurel leaves
  - => 1 tsp Cinnamon
  - => pinch black pepper
  - => 2 tbs. of dried dates
  - => 2 tbs. of dried raisins
  - => 2 tbs. licorice.

  => With a mortar and pestle crush everything except dates and raisins into a powder. Press this through a cloth to make fine powder. Crush dates and raisins and mix with powder to form a fine paste. Add honey to make a thick paste.
  => Roll in your palm to make small lozenges. Dry in the shade.
  => Will calm down the cough and clear voice.

- Recipe #2:
  => Ingredients:
    => 1 tsp. fresh ginger juice
    => 3 semi – crushed black pepper
    => 2 tsp. honey.
  => Mix and take twice daily. Beneficial to take at night before going to bed.

Chronic Dry Cough and Asthma

- There are two *yoga positions* that help. These are: **Serpent posture** and the **forward stretching posture**. Do these twice a day – first thing in the morning and last thing before going to bed.
- Do pranayama (breathing exercise) regularly. Do as much as you can, especially if breathing is difficult.
- Sniff something like pepper to induce sneezing.
- Follow a diet for reducing the **MOVEMENT energy** in the body. This concentrates on sweet, sour, salty foods. When you follow a diet for a specific remedy, it is important to remember that it is throwing your internal balance off. Therefore, follow it for as short a time as possible and then return to your regular routine. This diet includes:

RECOMMENDED FOODS

Vegetables

Asparagus	Okra (cooked)
Beets	Radishes
Carrots	Sweet potatoes
Cucumber	Turnips
Onions & Garlic (not raw)	Green beans

Fruits

Avocados	Bananas
Apricots	Berries
Figs	Coconut
Dates	
Grapes	Cherries
Lemons	Grapefruit
Nectarines	Mango
Oranges	Melons
Pineapple	Papayas
Stewed fruits	Peaches
Sweet, well – ripened fruit in general	

Grains

Oats (as cooked, oatmeal   Rice
cereal, not dry)
Wheat

Dairy

All are fine, in moderation

Meat

Chicken & Turkey   Seafood in general
(white meat)
All are acceptable in small
quantities

Oils

Sesame oil is the best   Generally, all oils are good

Herbs & Spices

Allspice   Anise
Basil   Bay Leaf
Caraway   Cardamom
Cilantro (green coriander) Cinnamon
Clove   Cumin
Fennel   Ginger
Licorice root   Marjoram
Mustard   Nutmeg
Oregano and Sage   Tarragon
Thyme
All, in moderation, with emphasis on
sweet or heating herbs and spices

Sweeteners

All are acceptable

Nuts and Seeds

Almonds are the best choice
Since the MOVEMENT force needs oil,
all oils are acceptable in small quantities

Legumes (Beans)

Chickpeas	Mung beans
Pink lentils	Tofu (in small amounts)

Generally legumes are gaseous which aggravates the ether component of the MOVEMENT force.

Blocked Nose

- Use the following mixture either as a poultice or add it to a bowl of steaming water, cover the head and inhale. (These items are available at a drugstore or a health food store.)
  => 5 parts eucalyptus oil
  => 1 part anise oil
  => 1 part menthol crystals
  => 2 part camphor

Congestion

Congestion is usually caused by an imbalance of the STORAGE energy force. Foods that help reduce the congestion include foods that are *pungent, astringent and bitter.* Eat as much of these foods as possible until the congestion clears.

Vegetables

Generally, all vegetables are good

	Asparagus
Beets	Broccoli
Brussels Sprouts	Cabbage
Carrots	Cauliflower
Celery	Eggplant
Garlic	Leafy green vegetables
Lettuce	Mushrooms
Okra	Onions
Peas	Peppers
Potatoes	Radishes
Spinach	Sprouts

Fruits

Apples   Apricots
Berries   Cherries
Cranberries   Peaches
Generally, All dried fruits are good

Grains

Barley   Buckwheat
Corn   Millet
Oats (dry)   Rice (basmati in small amounts)
Rye

Dairy

Skim milk and minimum   Boiled or poached
whole milk   eggs

Oils

Almond   Corn
Safflower   Sunflower

Meat

Chicken   Shrimp
Turkey
(all in small amounts)

Sweeteners

Raw, unheated honey

Nuts and Seeds

Sunflower seeds

Herbs and Spices

All spices are good   Ginger is best for improving digestion

Migraines

Migraines are usually caused by excess **MOVEMENT energy,** and sometimes an imbalance of fire in the body. Observe what is happening in your life and to your *prior* to getting a migraine. This is often the best method of controlling. When we learn what will trigger the headache *in our body*, then we can manage the warnings. Some things that trigger a migraine are:

- Physical fatigue
- Mental stress and/or fear
- Minor indigestion
- Irregular eating habits and heavy meals
- Loud noise, too much activity

Steps to help

1. DO NOT do your regular exercise, yoga or other form of exercise when you are tired or feel a migraine is coming.
2. Drink plenty of water.
3. Eat light meals **at regular times**.
4. Avoid fatty, heavy, fried foods.
5. Get a massage, followed by a bath (*sandalwood oil is beneficial*).
6. Practice Yoga breathing exercises, *pranayama* (approach this cautiously if you sense a headache approaching).
7. Meditate.
8. Avoid drinking alcohol in excess. Dry, sour wines, red wine, and strong drinks such as whiskey can precipitate a migraine.
9. Follow a diet that is **light and warm,** with **sweet, sour and salty** tastes. This is a MOVEMENT energy force diet.

PMS and Menstrual Symptom

If the reader is wondering why I singled out this ailment out of the many possible choices, it is because of the impact on everyone. Most women suffer some of PMS and Menstrual symptoms at some time in their lives. Men may not actually experience the physical and emotional effects but they still suffer because they have to relate to people who are distressed. A compassionate man will want to help.

The symptoms affect all three energy forces, regardless of which one is dominant. The list of ailments below shows two categories. The first column names symptoms of premenstrual discomforts. The second column is the menstrual imbalances. They are divided into the three energy forces so the reader can apply any balancing method to bring the energies back into balance. For example, if a person is suffering from fluid retention, the appropriate action is to follow a STORAGE balancing diet. This helps reduce the retention. It may not eliminate the difficulty completely, but it certainly helps. In future months, they may want to focus their attention on their diet just prior to the time when the symptoms appear.

MOVEMENT Energy

Premenstrual	**Mentrual**
Forgetful	Painful joints
Anxiety, insecurity	Cramps
Insomia	Lighter flow
Constipation	Dark blood
Abdominal bloating	Irregular cycle
Painful joints	Longer – lasting periods
Mood swings	

Common to both premenstrual and menstrual
Lower – back pain

STORAGE Energy

Vaginal infections	Regular cycle
Breast enlarged and tender	Tiredness, lethargy, needs extra sleep
Fluid retention	Stiffness in back and joints
Blood light – colored	Clots in blood flow
Slow Digestion	Heavy menstrual flow
Weight gain	

Common to both premenstrual and menstrual

Craving for sweets
Feelings of possessiveness
Depression

PROCESSING Energy

Hot flushes	
Excessive body heat	Nipples sensitive to touch
Skin rashes	Menstrual flow heavy and longer lasting
Diarrhea or loose bowels	Bright – red blood
	More frequent periods
	(shorter intervals between)

Common to both premenstrual and Menstrual for PROCESSING energy

Anger, irritability
Headaches, especially migraines
Burning sensation in urethra

Six Steps to Ease PMS and Menstrual Cramps

1. Sip *small* amounts of hot water regularly during the day (this helps clear out toxins).
2. Do half an hour of exercise every day.
3. Lean toward an energy – force balancing diet (select according to your symptoms above).
4. Keep PROCESSING foods to a minimum.
5. Eat main meal for lunch and a light, early supper.
6. Take it easy. Reduce work load and get extra rest.

Nine secrets for easier periods

1. Get plenty of rest.
2. Favor your inward tendencies. Arrange schedule to have quieter times and rest breaks.
3. Minimize exercise.
4. Eat light.
5. Opt for quick showers (bathing in hot water increases flow).
6. Postpone intercourse.
7. RX for cramps – Take 1 tablespoon of Aloe Vera gel with two pinches for black pepper 3 times a day until cramps disappear.
8. Sip hot water
9. Pacify your MOVEMENT energy with warmth. Use warm sesame oil gently massage your abdomen and lower back.

Herbs to Help with Your Cycle

Raspberry – leaf tea – reduces STORAGE and PROCESSING energies while increasing the MOVEMENT force.

Hibiscus flowers – These make a delicious tea, hot or cold. Raspberry and hibiscus can be combined.

Ginger Tea – reduces MOVEMENT and STORAGE energies while increasing PROCESSING force.

Mugwort (tea or capsules)

Dong Quai regulates the menstrual cycle.

Toothache Treatment

Naturally, this does not preclude a visit to your dentist. However, until you can get to him or her, here is a simple remedy that usually eases the pain.

Avoid eating foods at extreme temperatures. Depending upon the severity, you may want to emphasize softer foods.

Apply a small amount of tea tree oil or clove oil onto the sore tooth or gum. A cotton swab is a good tool.

Place a small piece of natural, edible camphor on the painful tooth. The saliva will mix with the camphor, soothing the pain. **NOTE:** Make sure the camphor is natural, as the synthetic camphor is poisonous.

Sprained and Strained Ankles

Most first – aid books concentrate on wrapping the foot and elevating the leg. Yet, there are simple remedies that compliment the usual procedures.

Drink juice. Pineapple and pomegranate juice contain enzymes that are anti - irritant and anti – inflammatory.

If it is a *SPRAIN*: Make a paste of ½ teaspoon turmeric and ½ teaspoon of salt. Use cool water to make a paste.

If it is a *STRAIN:* Use the same paste to reduce the swelling but for a strain, use hot water.

Sore Throat

GARGLE: Mix one cup of hot water, ½ teaspoon of turmeric and ½ teaspoons of salt. Gargle twice a day.

HERBAL TEA: Boil your water and add an herbal mixture of 2 parts ginger, 2 parts cinnamon and 3 parts licorice.

Avoid dairy products and fermented foods.

Jet Lag

Before flying: Approximately one hour before take 2 capsules of ginger with a glass of water. If you can't buy the capsules, make your own with fresh, ground ginger. Health stores usually have empty capsules.

In flight: Drink 2 – 3 glasses of water for every hour that you are in flight. Dehydration can be a problem on long flights.

After flying: At your destination, rub sesame oil on your scalp and soles of your feet. Drink a hot cup of milk or water with principles of nutmeg and ginger.

Insomnia

Warm milk:
    Add a pinch of nutmeg
    Add crushed almonds, pinch of nutmeg
    And pinch of cardamom
    Mix milk ¼ cup of water and 1 clove of fresh, chopped garlic

Cherries:
    A handful of cherries will help sleep.

Tomato Juice:
- Drink the following late in the afternoon
- Add 2 teaspoons of natural sugar and 2 pinches of nutmeg to a cup of juice.

XIV. CHAKRAS & THE ENERGY FORCES

It won't be surprising to many to discover that there is a close link between the chakra system and Ayurveda; quite naturally, since these methods both originated in India. But what is not as obvious is the specific link between the chakras and the energy forces of nature.

The seven main chakras of our body are gateways for the life force, or *prana.* What are the energy forces of Ayurveda but the life force divided into three pieces? Some time ago, I learned of a comparison placing a chakra in each of the curves of our spines. Since the spine is a main nerve channel in our body, it seems logical that the three Ayurveda energy forces would use the spine as its main highway. The MOVEMENT Force governs bones and nerves, both contained in the spine. This force is also responsible for pushing the PROCESSING and STORAGE forces throughout the body. Before we can look at the link between these two systems, we need a rudimentary understanding of each chakra, its main function and areas of the bodies connected to each. Each chakra has a specific colour assigned to it and it is through the colour that we will see the correlation. The seven chakras are:

Base, or root: As the name implies, it is the foundation of the emotional and mental health of the person. It governs the base of the spine, legs, bones, feet and the immune system. The colour is *RED.*

Second, or sacrum: This is your personal power centre for control and survival. It governs the large intestine, bladder, hipbones and lower vertebrae of the spine. The colour is *ORANGE.*

Third, or solar plexus: This is the centre of your intellect and your personal honour. It is through this chakra that your boundaries are identified. It governs the stomach, liver, kidney, liver, pancreas and adrenal glands, all the internal organs of the abdominal area. The colour is *YELLOW.*

Fourth, or heart: This chakra is the middle chakra of the body, balancing the lower chakras, the physical body, and the upper chakras, the spiritual. It governs the area of the upper body, heart, circulatory system, lungs, shoulders and thymus gland. The colour is *GREEN.*

Fifth, or throat: This is the communication chakra. It governs the communication between two humans, as well as trusting your guidance. The physical area it governs is the throat area, including thyroid and hypothalamus glands, the mouth and upper digestive track. The colour is *BLUE.*

Sixth, or third eye: This is the energy centre of our mind, both reasoning and intuition. It governs our nervous system, eyes and ears as well as the pituitary gland. The colour is *INDIGO.*

Seventh, or crown: Our connection with the spiritual world allows us to integrate our entire being. It governs the muscular and skeletal systems. The colour is *PURPLE or VILOET.*

Usually when the conversation turns to clearing our chakras, we follow methods developed through various energy health schools. What is forgotten is a circular loop. We can clear them by balancing our energy forces. We can balance our unique constitution by clearing our chakras. It is difficult to have one without the other.

If the flow of these forces is NOT clear and even, then the chakras become muddy and sluggish. Conversely, if the chakras are blocked for whatever reason, it spills over into the energy forces of the entire body. Both the energy worker and the Ayurvedic practitioner see the same symptoms; they just respond differently. The following section shows the correlation of the chakras, energy forces and colours. Although my research did not produce a great deal of information, the logic connecting these two is so exciting that it cannot be ignored.

Putting the Two Forces Together

As I looked at these two systems, I realized we needed a common denominator. Both can be described as flowing and vibrating. Colour vibrates, suggesting a possible link. To be successful, I needed to match the energy forces with the chakras and check to see if the associated chakra colours would, in fact, bring the energy forces into balance. The prime objective is to have the colours of each chakra, clear and bright. When the colour falls short of this, then it needs to be brightened up or energized. If the colour is TOO bright, then it needs to be calmed down.

The MOVEMENT energy force resides in the large intestine, pelvic cavity, bones, skin, nervous system and ears. The first two chakras are in this region and the 6th chakra governs the ears and nervous system. According to chakra balancing, we use red, orange and indigo. Ayurveda teachings tells us that red and indigo stimulate the energies which are good for a sluggish chakra. Orange is neutral. If the energy is too active, then colour would not be a good choice.

The PROCESSING energy force resides in the small intestine, stomach, eyes and blood. The 3rd, 4th and 6th chakras are all connected to this energy force. Therefore, balancing colours should be yellow, green and indigo. Ayurveda teachings tell us that yellow can aggravate this energy and so should be used sparingly. This is the one energy force that you don't want to intensify unnecessarily. It tolerates minor reductions in activity, but not minor increase. However, green and indigo are very compatible, excellent for these three chakras and this energy force. Blue can be used in moderation but with caution.

After discovering these correlations, I next looked at the colours from the chakra connection. If someone is adept at seeing or sending the colours then this is a useful and uncomplicated remedy.

We know that colour clears the chakras. We know that food, nature and exercise balance our energy forces. We have seen that there is a match between the chakras and the energy forces. Therefore, is it not logical that colour will do the same for both? Colours vibrate at diverse rates as do the three energy forces and the swirling energy of the chakras.

Matching the sluggish chakra and the tipped energy force with the appropriate colour is the task. We could incorporate *all* of the colours into our surroundings. And most of the time we would be all right. However, we do need to be aware of the traits of each colour and how we go about using them. We can then make minor adjustments toward harmony. Adding colour to our cupboard of cures gives us the options of food, exercise, colour and clearing of the chakras.

XV. COLOUR: THE POSITIVE INFLUENCE

There are two effortless methods for using colour as a balancing tool.

The first way is to wear seven small ribbons, each a different colour of the spectrum. This maintains the status quo of a balanced body. When you feel or sense a need for realignment, then a specific colour should dominate. You can either remove all the ribbons except the required colour or continue wearing them all with the designated colour a larger size.

The second method is more effective but takes time to prepare. Since the colours vibrate, wrap a piece of coloured transparent paper around a glass of pure water, making it suitable for drinking. This method is not dissimilar to the principle of flower essence preparation.

The colour descriptions below indicate which energy forces relate to which one. It is important, though, to understand that it is the intensity of the colour that tells us just how much balancing or clearing it will do. For example, when we look at a chakra, we want to see purity of colour. When we are balancing the energy forces, we need to soften this, otherwise we risk pushing the balance way over to the other side.

Since the **MOVEMENT** energy is cold and light, you need a hot, stimulating colour, one associated with movement. Unless, of course, you are trying to calm it down. This is an example of slightly altering the intensity of a colour. Changing red into pink is an example. Two colours that increase the MOVEMENT energy are red and indigo. A colour that slows the MOVEMENT down is yellow.

The **PROCESSING** energy force requires colours that are cool, light and calming to achieve balance. Two colours that reduce the force are green and blue. When choosing a colour it is important to remember the counter – effects of a colour. By this, I mean that if you use too intense a colour or too much of it, the desired effect is lost.

The **STORAGE** force needs something to get things moving – colours that are light. Two colours that increase this energy are blue and green. Two colours that will reduce it are red and yellow.

RED

Red is one of the warmest colours. It is stimulating, and so encourages MOVEMENT. It is also one of the hottest colours and, since it is associated with the blood and nerves, it is useful for bones and digestive movement. However, since it aggravates the 'fire' in the body, it may upset the PROCESSING, so it must be used carefully. If your body needs to reduce both MOVEMENT and PROCESSING forces, then red is acceptable, providing it is not used excessively. An alternative solution might be pink, since it is warming but is also calming.

ORANGE

Orange carries many of the same properties as Red. It is warm, healing and stimulating, therefore a good MOVEMENT and STORAGE remedy. STORAGE people need more love and attention when they are out of balance. Potentially, it may upset the balance of PROCESSING. It is useful as an antibacterial, as it hinders the growth.

YELLOW

Yellow is linked to the crown chakra – mental and spiritual intelligence. In addition, it is the colour of the bile of our stomach. Therefore, it aids in the MOVEMENT of thought. When there is excess bile in the stomach, yellow will throw the body out of balance even more. It is useful in reducing congestion in the throat area.

GREEN

Green is calming, cool colour, therefore is a useful colour to reduce the PROCESSING energy. It is an effective cleanser of the heart chakra. It increases the other two energy forces.

BLUE

Blue is most effective for calming the PROCESSING energy. When it is used in excess, it can increase the other two energy forces.

PURPLE

When there is a need to *lighten* the body, then this is the best colour remedy. Since MOVEMENT involves air and ether, caution is important. The energy force that benefits the most is the STORAGE energy force.

XVI. MASSAGE

Ayurvedic massage differs from therapeutic massage.

The latter is the popular massage in North America. Some of this style's benefits include:

- Bringing muscles back to normal function.
- Increasing circulation
- Enhancing athletic performance
- Working on the nervous system to reduce pain
- Returning muscles and fascia to normal function

Ayurvedic massage's role is slightly different. There are three purposes to this method:

- Removing toxins in the system.
- Creating a balance of the three energy forces.
- Improving circulation.

Quite naturally, the first action is identify the dominant energy force. This allows the practitioner to prepare the appropriate oils, since each force requires different attributes. All three are achieved by infusing the best herbs into the appropriate oil. For each dominant force, There are ideal oils, times of day and techniques. Some general tips are:

- Keep a bottle of medicated oil near your shower.
- After the shower, pour some of the oil on a dry cloth and rub it over your entire body or put it directly into the palm of your hand.
- Stroking against the grain of the body hairs helps the penetration of the oil.
- Whenever possible, use non – hydrogenated, cold – pressed oils. These should be kept in the refrigerator once opened.
- Fresh herbs are the best for the body, dried as a second choice.
- For poor circulation, massage toward the heart.
- For muscle spasms or soreness, massage in the direction of the muscle fibers.

MOVEMENT – dominant people have dry skin and they simply love all the oil that is available. The best base oil is sesame oil, almond oil. Their massage should be gentle since this force is very high energy. Even though the optimum time for this massage is in the evening, when this force is high, giving a self – massage after the shower improves circulation. The massage oil and the herbs will not aggravate this energy force at this time.

PROCESSING – dominant people require cooling medicated oil. For these people, **sunflower** or **sandalwood** oil – base cools their body. Since they also tend to be dry, but not as dry as the MOVEMENT – dominant person, they also benefit from the shower massage. The best time for them is afternoon – not easy in a busy Western schedule. Again, since these people are high energy, The massage should be gentle.

STORAGE – dominant people need either a light oil massage or a dry herbal massage. Their best oil – base is **corn oil** or **Calamus root**. Calamus Root (Sweet Flag) is considered toxic by some and therefore should be used cautiously. It is, however, a very effective remedy for nervous disorders. We need to remember that our skin is one of the best gateways into our system. The best time for these people is in the morning. Ironically, they benefit from a deep massage, not a gentle shower rub.

Making the Oil

There are many ways to prepare the oil. Each practitioner or herbalist has their favourite. This method was given to me by a dear friend, Marilyn Dyke, both an herbalist and spiritualist. Whether the herb is fresh or dry, this gives you medicated oil that is ready in about 2 weeks and lasts for approximately one year in the refrigerator. This recipe produces a thick, strongly coloured paste. However, once it is strained, it has the same consistency as the plain oil. It is best to apply it to the palm of the hand and then rub gently over the body.

Some herbalists will add a small amount of alcohol. While it doesn't destroy the properties, it does weaken the strength of the oil.

- Combine in a blender: one part herb, not the root, and 7 parts of desired oil. Select the oil according to the energy force.
- If you are using a fresh plant, you must let it sit on a towel for a few hours. This is to wilt the plant and remove some of the moisture content. It is the water that makes the oil go rancid very fast. If you bypass this step, it could go rancid very fast. If you bypass this step, it could go rancid even before the 2 weeks maceration process is over.
- Blend on high until the sides of the container feel almost too hot to touch.
- Pour into a glass jar, cover and place in the dark for about 2 weeks. Vigorously shake the mixture twice daily. This step is called maceration.
- If you want a stronger mixture, repeat the process, replacing the oil with the herbal blend and adding a small amount of herb.
- Strain into a clean jar. If you have used fresh herbs, you must let the strained oil stand for a while and then decant the oil layer off the water layer. Any water left in the oil makes it go rancid. Store in the refrigerator.

For a massage for a STORAGE – dominant person, the best way to apply the herbs is through a dry massage. Simply combine the powdered or crushed herbs and sprinkle onto the skin. Then with dry hands, massage it into the skin. The herbs will gradually be absorbed into the body.

NOTE: If you can't store it in the refrigerator, add grapefruit seed extract to prevent it from going rancid. Use the ratio of 5 drops of grapefruit seed extract per 30ml (1 Oz.) of oil.

Twenty Herbs Found In Your Kitchen

For a complete selection, I suggest referring to an herb book such as **Yoga of Herbs** by Vasant Lad and David Frawley. To get you started, use the following herbs found in your kitchen. For the energy force, I have used the first letter "M, P, S", "-, +, =" to indicate whether they reduce, increase or maintain the amount of the force. I have selected the main actions for each herb according to Ayurveda philosophy.

Herb	Energy Force	Action
Alfalfa	PS-, M+	Astringent, diuretic
Aloe Vera	All =, P= slightly	Rejuvenative
Bay leaves	MS-, P+	Improves Digestion
Calamous Root	MS-, P+	Stimulant, decongestant
Cardamom	MS-, P+	Improves digestion expectorant
Chamomile	PS-, M+	Perspiration' improves digestion
Chickweed	PS-, M+	*Alternative, demulcent
Cinnamon	MS-, P+	`Stimulant, Alterative
Coriander	MPS-	Alterative improves digestion
Echinacea	PS-, M+	Alterative antibiotic
Flax seed	M-, SP+	Laxative, demulcent
Garlic	M,S-,P+	Stimulant, improves digestion
Ginger	M, S-, P+	Perspiration, expectorant
Gotu kola	MPS=	Nerves, alterative
Licorice Root	MP-, S+	Protects membranes, tonic
Mustard	SM-, P+	Stimulant,

		expectorant
Nutmeg	MS-, P+	Sedative, nerves and digestion
Onion	MS, P+	Perspiration, tonic
Turmeric	S-, PM+	Antibacterial, stimulant
Yellow Dock	PS-, M+	Alterative, astringent

*An alterative helps restore normal health, cleanses and purifies the blood. A demulcent protects internal membranes.

XVII. EXERCISE

When searching for an ideal exercise, it is important to consider the cycles of life whenever possible.

According to the *daily* cycle of time, the best times to exercise is first thing in the thing in the morning, before breakfast. This is when the STORAGE energy is relaxed and calm and can tolerate the activity. Exercise later in the day when the MOVEMENT and PROCESSING are high will simply cause imbalances.

The *seasons* are easier to plan around since we can each select three exercise routines and rotate them according to the season.

The PROCESSING – dominant people will want to avoid exercise during the heat of summer. They would be better to practice yoga or cool walks in the early mornings during the summer months.

Late winter and early spring are the seasons when the STORAGE energy is open to aggravation; their exercise at this time needs to be in a dry, warm location. They risk the danger of colds and congestion.

MOVEMENT people need to avoid the cold and winds of winter. Any exercise that is indoors is beneficial for them.

The last cycle we need to be aware of is the *moon*. Although we do need to exercise regularly, we don't want to upset the forces that follow the moon's cycle.

When the moon is full, the energy is heavy and dense. This increases the STORAGE energy within our body. When the moon is new, the energy is light but intense. This reminds us of the PROCESSING energy. Therefore, this is a time when this energy would be increased.

My previous book, INNER BRIDGES, has more information about the cycles and ways to balance the body. Since its emphasis is not the energy forces of life, it does not specifically correlate the cycles with each energy force. However, after the introduction and use the information given.

Each energy force has exercises that are ideal. Selecting the exercise according to your dominant pattern will allow you to make minor changes according to your favourite pastime.

The **MOVEMENT – dominant** person has bursts of energy and tire easily. Therefore, the best exercises are: walking, swimming (in clean lakes not in chlorinated water!), bicycling, yoga or Tai chi. These people excel at balancing and stretching activities.

The **PROCESSING – dominant** person has a lot of drive and only a moderate amount of endurance. For them, the best exercise are: skiing, brisk walking or jogging, hiking, and mountain climbing.

The **STORAGE – dominant** person has the endurance and stamina all envy. therefore, their exercise regime should include weight training, running (long distance), aerobics, and rowing.

XVIII. CONCLUSION

Cultures elsewhere on earth spent thousands of years studying the cycles of life and, based on this, developed an ideal healthy lifestyle. We now have the advantage of taking the best out each one and incorporating it into Western living.

Our current medical practices only go back to the seventeenth century. Ayurveda and Chinese medicines go back 5,000 years. The North American indigenous studies go just as far, if not farther. The Japanese adopted the Chinese method in the sixth century and named it *kampo*. Why then shouldn't we incorporate ancient knowledge into our scientific knowledge? This small book does just that. When the individual takes care of daily activities, routine cycles, minor imbalances and the scientific doctors are able to take care of major ailments much more easily & when a Western doctor has to treat a body, it is easier to work with a normally healthy one.

Once we understand the flow of energy forces pervading our lives, we can then make conscious choices.

I realize that it is not always possible to modify our lifestyle. So much of Western living and business dictates how we live. However, any effort we make helps maintain our health an overall well-being. Our bodies are designed to last a long time; we just need to know how to care for them. A car that never gets an oil change won't last long. A body that is ignored, won't last long, either.

Recently I discovered a difference between partial truths and half - truths. For me, a *partial truth* is a statement or tale that contains as much information as an individual can absorb at a particular time. *Half - truths*, on the other hand, are small pieces of information doled out by a person with the intent of control or power. This book is a partial truth. It is intended to introduce the concepts of Ayurveda to the reader with a Western approach. The next step would be to read one of the books in the bibliography. I encourage everyone to do so. Until then, review the following pages. These summarize the traits of each energy force and the general tips od Ayurveda.

Summary of the Recognizable Traits for Each Dominant Energy Forces

As we have said before, each person is unique and has a personal blend of energy forces. If we could quantify each, we might see a countless array of percentages. Even memebers of the same family or race will differ. As we look at the traits, this becomes more apparent. A trait such as *dryness* has degress of definition. What is dry to one person is not always dry to another.

When we begin observing others, it is almost impossible to mentally record everything about an individual. An effective alternative is to make a personal shortlist of our favourite indicators. The following is a summary of attributes to choose from. It also gives us a checklist for ourselves.

MOVEMENT dominance

- **Dry** — Dry skin, hair, lips, tongue, hoarse voice, dry colon which leads toward constipation.
- **Light** — Light muscles, boness, thin body frame, light scanty sleep, prone to underweight.
- **Cold** — Cold hands, feet, poor circulation hates cold and loves hot; stiffness of muscles.
- **Rough** — Rough, cracked skin, nails, hair, teeth, hands and feet, cracking joints.
- **Subtle** — Subtle fear, anxiety, insecurity, pimples, minute muscle twitching, fine tremors, delicate body.
- **Mobile** — Fast walking, talking, doing many things at a time, restless eyes, unstable joints, many dreams, loves travelling but does not stay at one place, moods swings.
- **Clear** — Clairvoyant understands quickly and forgets immediately, clear, open mind, experiences void and loneliness.
- **Astringent** — Dry, choking sensation in the throat, gets hiccoughs, burping, loves oil, mushy foods, craving for sweet, sour and salty tastes.

PROCESSING dominance

- **Hot** — Good digestive fire, strong appetite, body temperature tends to be higher than normal, hates heat, early gray hair with receding hairline or baldness.
- **Sharp** — Sharp teeth, distinct eyes, pointed nose, tapering chin, heart - shaped face, good absorption and digestion; sharp memory and understanding; irritable moods.
- **Light** — Light/medium body frame; does not tolerate bright light, fair shiny skin, bright eyes.
- **Oily** — Soft oily skin, hair, does not like deep - fried food (which may cause headaches).
- **Liquid** — Loose liquid stools, soft delicate muscles; excess sweat and thirst.
- **Sour** — Sour acidic stomach and pH; sensitive teeth; excess salivation.
- **Bitter** — Bitter taste in mouth, nausea, vomiting, cycnical.
- **Fleshy smell** — Strong odor under armpits, mouth, soles of feet; smelly socks.
- **Ruddy** — Red flushed skin, cheeks and nose.
- **Yellow** — Yellow eyes, skin, urine, many led to jaundice, overproduction of bile.

STORAGE dominance

- **Damp, Cool** — Clammy skin, a steady appetite, repeated colds and congestion.
- **Heavy** — Large bones and body frame, tends to be overweight, deep heavy voice.
- **Slow** — Walking, talking and metabolism in general.
- **Oily** — Skin and hair.
- **Dense** — Fat, thick hair, skin and nails.
- **Smooth** — Skin, calm nature.
- **Soft** — Compassionate voice, soft skin.
- **Sedentary** — Loves doing nothing.
- **Cloudy** — Needs time to focus and start moving.
- **Flavours** — Pungent, astringent and bitter tasting foods.

- Healthy joints Indicates a balanced energy.

Last minute Tips

"Like increases like." Therefore, we want to include activities that will NOT increase the enrgy function that is dominant at a specific time of day. Therfore:

- Our STORAGE - dominant time is early morning so we want include activities that will NOT agravate it. Exercise and getting up early are best for this energy force.
- PROCESSING is at its peak around noon. This is when we want to utilize the efficiency of digestion. Eat your big meal of the day this time.
- MOVEMENT is night - time and early afternoon. This is when we need to rest and counteract the effects of the nervous/movement energy in our bodies.

Amadea Morningstar notes: [2]

> "*(Ayurveda) offers us a clear system of concepts and principles, an understanding of natural laws which is invaluable to us at this time, as we struggle to birth a planetary culture and face the consequences of our years of mispractice and neglect of the planet and natural law*"

---

[2] Morningstar, Amadea, *The Ayurvedic Cookbook*, Lotus Press Wisconsin 1990

There is a growing and urgent need to blend all the information and help that is available to us. Ayurveda offers us a lifestyle system that we can easily adopt without sacrificing our Western values. It is a way that we can manage our own health and reduce the pressure on out health care system.

XIX. INDEX

A

acidophilus, 61, 99

age, 14–16, 25, 36, 51, 99

alfalfa, 90, 99

almond oil, 53, 88, 99. *See also* oils

aloe vera, 78, 99

anger, 21–22, 28, 34, 66–67, 77, 99

asthma, 21, 35, 60, 63, 70, 99

astringent, 27, 34, 36, 44–45, 47–48, 60–61, 63–64, 73, 90–91, 95, 97, 99

Ayurvedic Cookbook, The (Morningstar), 97

Ayurvedic massage, 87

B

balance, 3, 7–8, 10–13, 16–17, 20, 34, 36–37, 39, 41, 48, 70, 76, 82–85, 87, 92

butter, 43, 46–47, 50, 54, 59, 61–62, 68–69, 99

buttermilk, 61

C

calamus, 88, 99

camphor, 73, 79, 99

cankers, 67, 99

cardamom, 38, 43, 47, 60, 68–69, 72, 80, 90, 99

cardinal, 12, 99

castor oil, 64. *See also* oils

chakra, 81–86, 99

chamomile, 67, 90, 99

cholesterol, 21–22, 35, 43, 61–62, 99

cinnamon, 43, 47, 66, 68–69, 72, 79, 90, 99

colour, 25, 27, 61, 81–86, 99

congestion, 35, 67, 73, 85, 92, 96, 99

coriander, 43, 47, 67, 72, 90, 99

corn oil, 54. *See also* oils

cranberry juice, 67, 99

D

daily cycle, 14, 92, 99

dairy, 42, 46, 49, 54, 59–60, 71, 74, 79, 99

demulcent, 90–91, 99

depression, 32, 35, 66, 77

diet, 5, 7, 10, 20, 29, 33–34, 36–38, 66–67, 70, 75–77, 99

diuretic, 90, 99

Dong Quai, 78, 99

E

echinacea, 90, 99

elements, 7, 16, 99

energy forces, 11, 13–16, 19–23, 32, 45, 48, 50–51, 60–61, 63, 66, 76, 81–84, 86–90, 92–95, 97

exercise, 3, 16, 36, 66, 75, 77–78, 83, 92–93, 97

expectorant, 90–91, 99

eyes, 20, 23–24, 27, 29–30, 62–64, 82–83, 95–96, 99

F

face, 24, 96, 99

flax seed, 90, 99

Frawley, David, 90

Yoga of Herbs, 90

XX. BIBLIOGRAPHY

Recommended list for further studies:

Note: When doing comparative studying

MOVEMENT Function = VATA,
PROCESSING Function = PITTA,
STORAGE Function = KAPHA

- Anselmo & James Brooks, *Ayurvedic Secrets to LOngevity & Total Health*, Prentice Hall, New Jersey, 1996
- Chopra, Deepak, *Perfect Health, the Complete Mind/Body Guide*, Harmony Books, New York, 1991
- Lad, Vasant, *The Complete Book Of Ayurvedic Home Remedie*s, Three Rivers Press, New York, 1998
- Lad, Dr. Vasant, *Ayurveda, The Science of Self-Healing*, Lotus Light, Wisconsin, 1984
- Frawley, Dr. David and Lad, Dr. Vasant, *Yoga of Herbs*, Lotus Press, Wisconsin, 1986
- Miller, Light and Bryan Miller, *Ayurveda & Aromatherapy*, Lotus Press, Wisconsin, 1995
- Morningstar, Amadea, and Urmila Desai *The Ayurvedic Cookbook*, Lotus Press, Wisonsin 1990
- Ros, Frank Dr., *The Lost Secrets of Ayurvedic Acupuncture*, Lotus Press, Wisconsin, 1994
- Svoboda, Robert E, *Prakruti, Your Ayurvedic Constitution*, Geocom, New Mexico, 1989
- Verma, Vinod Dr., *Ayurveda, A Way of Life*, Samuel Weiser, Inc., Maine, 1995

www.ingramcontent.com/pod-product-compliance
Lightning Source LLC
Chambersburg PA
CBHW080522030726

47592CB00012B/3438